20 QUESTIONS: Earth Science

What Do You Know About Rocks?

PowerKiDS press
New York

Gillian Gosman

Published in 2014 by The Rosen Publishing Group, Inc.
29 East 21st Street, New York, NY 10010

Copyright © 2014 by The Rosen Publishing Group, Inc.

All rights reserved. No part of this book may be reproduced in any form without permission in writing from the publisher, except by a reviewer.

First Edition

Editor: Jennifer Way
Book Design: Kate Laczynski

Photo Credits: Cover Daniel Osterkamp/Flickr/Getty Images; cover/interior graphic risteski goce/Shutterstock.com; p. 5 © iStockphoto.com/Deborah Cheramie; p. 6 Jody Amiet/Stringer/AFP/Getty Images; p. 7 Nerdist72/Shutterstock.com; p. 8 © iStockphoto.com/Brendan Hunter; p. 9 (top) Steven Kaufman/Peter Arnold/Getty Images; p. 9 (bottom) John Cancalosi/Oxford Scientific/Getty Images; p. 10 (top) © iStockphoto.com/Tyler Boyes; p. 10 (bottom) kojihirano/Shutterstock.com; p. 11 (top) Robert Crow/Shutterstock.com; p. 11 (bottom) © iStockphoto.com/Eirik Johan Solheim; pp. 12–13 Boykov/Shutterstock.com; p. 13 (bottom) vicspacewalker/Shutterstock.com; p. 15 Mary Terriberry/Shutterstock.com; p. 16 Martin M303/Shutterstock.com; p. 17 Iakov Kalinin/Shutterstock.com; p. 18 iStockphoto/Thinkstock; p. 19 Presniakov Oleksandr/Shutterstock.com; p. 20 Pecold/Shutterstock.com; p. 21 Jeff Fusco/Stringer/Getty Images News; p. 22 Marko5/Shutterstock.com.

Gosman, Gillian.
 What do you know about rocks? / by Gillian Gosman. — 1st ed.
    p. cm. — (20 questions. Earth science)
 Includes index.
 ISBN 978-1-4488-9696-7 (library binding) — ISBN 978-1-4488-9850-3 (pbk.) — ISBN 978-1-4488-9851-0 (6-pack)
 1. Petrology—Juvenile literature. 2. Rocks—Juvenile literature. I. Title.
 QE432.2.G674 2013
 552—dc23
                                    2012018695

Manufactured in the United States of America

CPSIA Compliance Information: Batch #S13PK5: For Further Information contact Rosen Publishing, New York, New York at 1-800-237-9932

Contents

What Do You Know About Rocks? 4
1. What do geologists study? 6
2. What is the rock cycle? 7
3. What are rocks made of? 8
4. What are minerals? 8
5. What are crystals? 9
6. What are the three types of rocks? 10
7. What is magma? 11
8. What are igneous rocks? 12
9. What are intrusive igneous rocks? 12
10. What are volcanic rocks? 13
11. What are metamorphic rocks? 14
12. How are metamorphic rocks formed? 15
13. What are examples of metamorphic rocks? 15
14. What is sediment? 16
15. What are sedimentary rocks and how do they form? 17
16. What are fossils? 18
17. How do fossils form in sedimentary rocks? 19
18. What is weathering? 20
19. What is erosion? 21
20. How can we prevent erosion caused by human activity? ... 22
Glossary 23
Index 24
Websites 24

What Do You Know About Rocks?

The rocks that make up our world are always changing. Slowly but surely, they are moving, melting, coming together, or breaking down.

Scientists study the processes by which rocks change. In the following chapters, you will learn about the rock cycle and what rocks are made of. You will explore the three kinds of rocks and learn how they form. You will see how rock records the past and discover how humans are making their own dangerous impact on the rock record. Get ready to dig deep!

By looking closely at rocks with a magnifying glass, you can often more easily tell what type of rock they are and what they are made of.

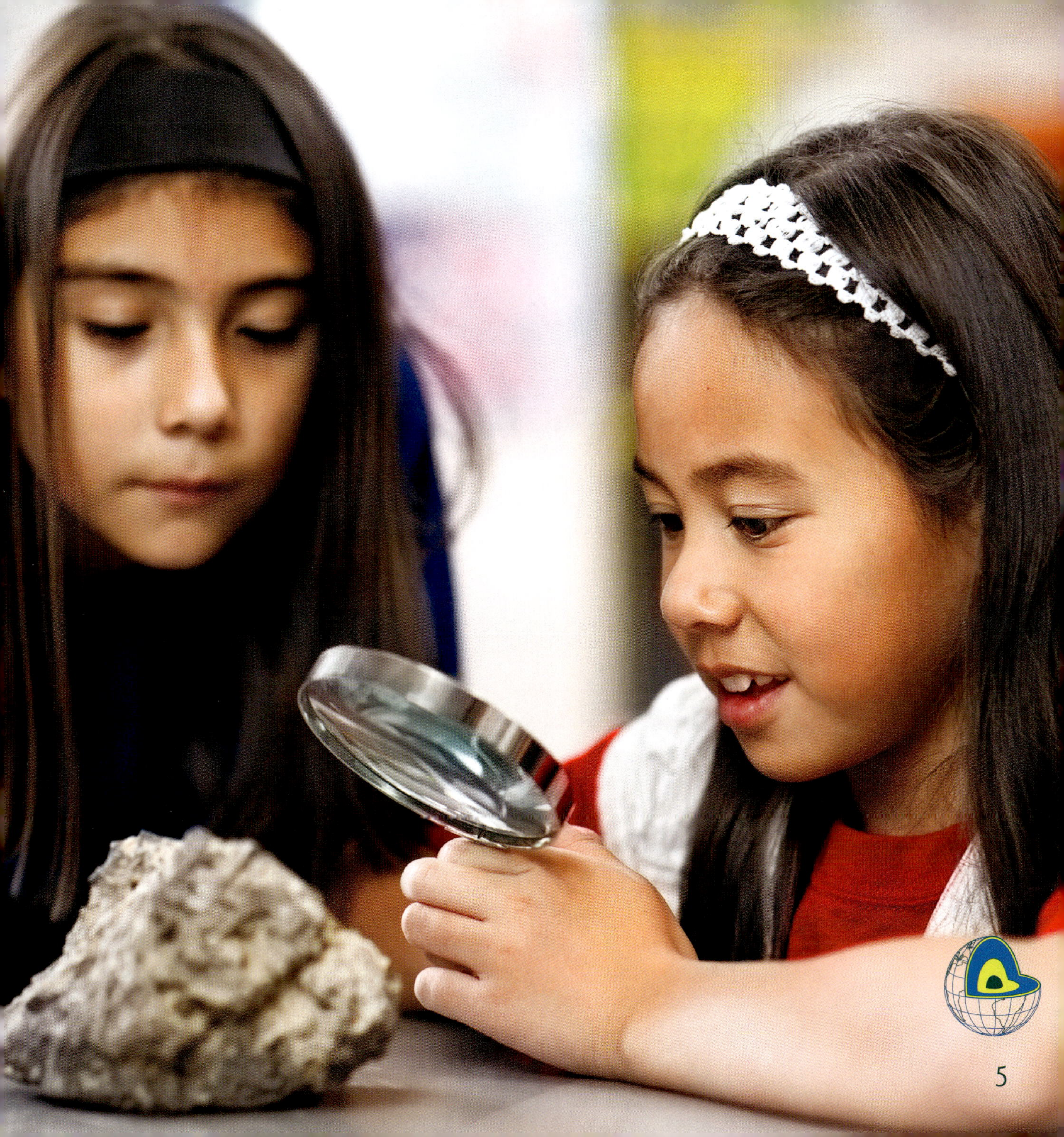

1. What do geologists study?

The history of Earth is billions of years long. Geologists are scientists who study this history. They study the planet's past so that they can understand the world today and predict, or guess, how Earth will change in the future. Geologists study things such as rocks, oil, water, and metals. They also study events such as earthquakes, floods, and the **eruptions** of volcanoes.

These geologists are looking at a rock to learn more about a storm that happened over 150 years ago!

2. What is the rock cycle?

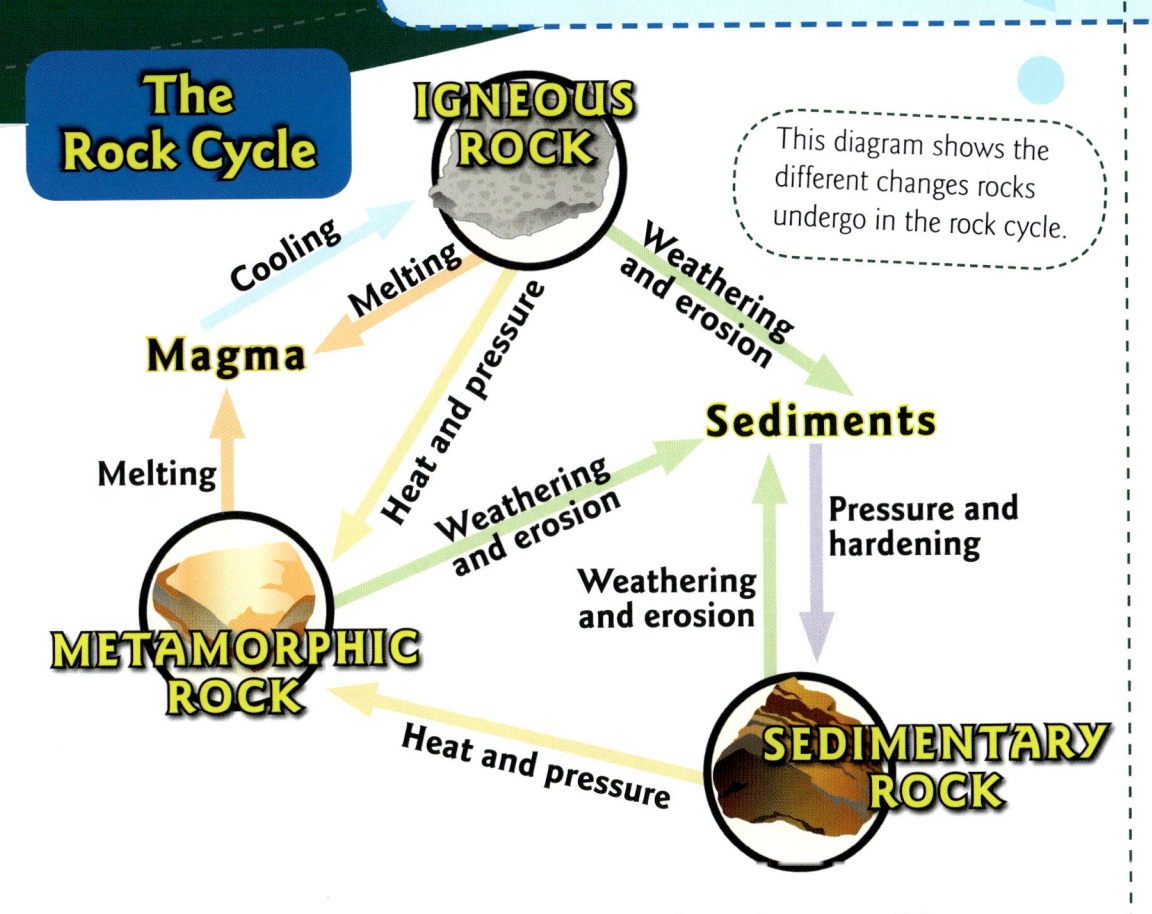

The Rock Cycle

This diagram shows the different changes rocks undergo in the rock cycle.

- IGNEOUS ROCK
- Cooling
- Melting
- Weathering and erosion
- Magma
- Heat and pressure
- Melting
- Weathering and erosion
- Sediments
- Pressure and hardening
- Weathering and erosion
- METAMORPHIC ROCK
- Heat and pressure
- SEDIMENTARY ROCK

Geologists also study how rocks change. The rock cycle describes the process of how rocks change from one form into another. Rocks change when they are heated, cooled, pressed down on, or broken down by wind or water.

7

3. What are rocks made of?

All rock is made up of two or more minerals.

This rock is partly made up of the mineral quartz.

4. What are minerals?

There are more than 3,000 different kinds of minerals on Earth. Each mineral is made up of a special chemical **structure**, which means it is the same material all through the mineral. In this way, minerals are different from rocks. A rock can be made up of many different minerals, so it is not the same substance all the way through.

5. What are crystals?

Crystals are minerals that have been allowed to grow according to their natural patterns. Every mineral has its own pattern for growth, and scientists can tell which mineral a crystal is by looking closely at its shape.

QUARTZ CRYSTALS

Malachite crystals often form in a globular pattern.

9

IGNEOUS ROCK

6. What are the three types of rocks?

There are three types of rocks. They are **igneous rocks**, **metamorphic rocks**, and **sedimentary rocks**. Their names describe the forces that formed the rocks. Rock formation is a long, slow process. It happens over thousands and even millions of years.

SEDIMENTARY ROCK

7. What is magma?

Here is lava flowing out of a volcano in Hawaii.

METAMORPHIC ROCK

Magma is a mixture of melted and mostly melted rock. It forms deep below Earth's crust, where temperatures reach 1,600° F (871° C). Magma often collects underground and is forced out through openings in Earth's crust, such as volcanoes. When it erupts from underground, magma is called lava.

11

8. What are igneous rocks?

Igneous rocks are formed when rock deep under the ground is heated to very high temperatures and melts, becoming magma. When the rock cools, it hardens. This hardened rock is igneous rock. There are two main kinds of igneous rocks.

9. What are intrusive igneous rocks?

Intrusive igneous rocks are formed when magma flows into cracks and open spaces below Earth's crust. As it moves, it slowly cools and hardens over the course of many thousands of years. Granite is a common intrusive igneous rock.

10. What are volcanic rocks?

Volcanic rocks are igneous rocks formed when magma escapes Earth's crust through openings called volcanoes. The melted rock reaches Earth's surface, cools, and hardens. Basalt and pumice are both volcanic rocks.

Mount Rushmore, shown here, is made of granite.

PUMICE

Seneca Rocks is a rock formation in West Virginia. It is made of quartzite, a type of metamorphic rock.

11. What are metamorphic rocks?

Metamorphic rocks are rocks that have changed form because of the movements of Earth's crust.

14

12. How are metamorphic rocks formed?

Earth's crust is broken into large pieces, called plates. Changes deep below Earth's crust cause the plates to move. When two or more plates come together, the rock that lies between them is pressed, while the magma below the crust heats it. The pressure and heat cause the rock to change.

13. What are examples of metamorphic rocks?

The most common metamorphic rock is called schist. It is made of several common minerals, including mica, graphite, and quartz. Marble is another very popular metamorphic rock. It is formed when limestone is pressed and heated.

14. What is sediment?

Sedimentary rocks are made of sediment. The water's **current** carries the sediment along until it finally settles at the bottom of an ocean, river, or stream. There, it is pressed together by the weight of the water, forming new layers of sediment. Over time, the sediment hardens and forms sedimentary rock.

The Grand Canyon, shown here, has many layers of sedimentary rock such as sandstone, shale, and limestone.

If you stand in the ocean, you might feel the sand moving with the water's current.

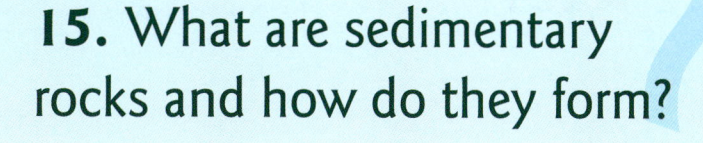

15. What are sedimentary rocks and how do they form?

Sediment is small pieces of rock and minerals that settle at the bottoms of oceans, rivers, and streams, along with mud, clay, and sand. In some areas, sediment also includes small pieces of once-living matter, such as shells, bones, and plant parts.

16. What are fossils?

Fossils are important because they give scientists information about the plants and animals that once lived on Earth but that died out long ago.

Sediment helps tell the story of Earth's past. Dead plant and animal matter can be trapped and preserved in layers of sediment. These preserved pieces of dead matter are called **fossils**.

17. How do fossils form in sedimentary rocks?

It is not easy to make a fossil. Most of the plants and animals that have lived on Earth simply die and decay, or break down. To make a fossil, a few things must take place. The dead plant or animal matter must be protected against weather, animals, and anything else that might help that matter decay. Next, sediment must settle on and around the dead thing. Finally, the sediment must harden into sedimentary rock.

FOSSILIZED FERN

18. What is weathering?

Rocks face all sorts of weather. Rain beats on them, and the wind races across them. Waves crash on the shore, and **glaciers** move across the land. Rainwater may collect in a crack in a rock during the day and freeze at night. When it freezes, the water expands, or takes up more space, causing the rock to crack open. Over time, these natural processes break down rock into smaller pieces. This process is called weathering.

Weathering created rock formations like those in Arches National Park, shown here.

19. What is erosion?

Erosion happens when small pieces of broken-down rock are blown by the wind or carried along by moving water. Wind and water carry the rock pieces away and deposit, or set down, the pieces somewhere else.

A storm caused the erosion shown on this New Jersey beach.

20. How can we prevent erosion caused by human activity?

Erosion is a natural process, but human activity can greatly speed up the process. When people clear plants from the land, it is left unprotected from erosion. Water and wind can then carry the soil away. This muddy sediment can cause landslides and **pollute** waterways. In addition, the land left behind is poor and may become desert. We can prevent erosion by planting trees and other plants that will hold the soil together, protecting it from weathering and erosion.

Terrace farming, shown here, is a special way that farmers can plant crops to protect the soil from erosion.

Glossary

current (KUR-ent) Water that flows in one direction.

eruptions (ih-RUP-shunz) The explosions of gases, smoke, or lava from volcanoes.

fossils (FO-sulz) The hardened remains of dead animals or plants.

glaciers (GLAY-shurz) Large masses of ice that move down mountains or along valleys.

igneous rocks (IG-nee-us ROKS) Hot, liquid, underground minerals that have cooled and hardened.

intrusive (in-TROO-siv) Referring to a type of igneous rock formed when magma cools and hardens under Earth's surface.

magma (MAG-muh) Hot, melted rock inside Earth.

metamorphic rocks (meh-tuh-MOR-fik ROKS) Rocks that have been changed by heat and heavy weight.

pollute (puh-LOOT) To hurt with certain kinds of bad matter.

sedimentary rocks (seh-deh-MEN-teh-ree ROKS) Stones, sand, or mud that has been pressed together to form rocks.

structure (STRUK-cher) Form.

Index

C
cycle, 4, 7

E
Earth, 6, 8, 19
eruptions, 6

F
fossil(s), 18–19
future, 6

G
geologists, 6–7
glaciers, 20

H
history, 6
humans, 4

I
igneous rock(s), 10, 12–13
impact, 4

K
kinds, 4, 8, 12

M
magma, 11–13, 15

O
oil, 6

P
past, 4, 6, 18

R
record, 4

S
scientists, 4, 6, 9
sediment, 16–19, 22
sedimentary rock(s), 10, 16, 19

Websites

Due to the changing nature of Internet links, PowerKids Press has developed an online list of websites related to the subject of this book. This site is updated regularly. Please use this link to access the list: www.powerkidslinks.com/20es/rock/